PRIMARY SOURCES IN AMERICAN HISTORY™

THE PONY EXPRESS
A PRIMARY SOURCE HISTORY OF THE RACE TO BRING MAIL TO THE AMERICAN WEST

SIMONE PAYMENT

rosen central
Primary Source™

The Rosen Publishing Group, Inc., New York

Published in 2005 by The Rosen Publishing Group, Inc.
29 East 21st Street, New York, NY 10010

Library of Congress Cataloging-in-Publication Data

Payment, Simone.
The Pony Express: A primary source history of the race to bring mail to the
    American west/by Simone Payment.—1st ed.
    p. cm.—(Primary sources in American history)
Includes bibliographical references and index.
Contents: Introduction: the Pony Express connects the country—Timeline—
Before the Pony Express—Planning the Pony Express—And they're off!—The
weekly ride—Hardships on the trail—The end of the ride.
ISBN 1-4042-0181-5 (library binding)
1. Pony express—History—Juvenile literature. 2. Postal service—United
States—History—Juvenile literature. [1. Pony express. 2. Postal service—
History.]
I. Title. II. Series: Primary sources in American history (New York, N.Y.)
HE6375.P65P396 2005
383'.143'0973—dc22

                                                                2003022268

Manufactured in the United States of America

On the front cover: *The Pursuit,* a lithograph issued from J. H. Bufford's Print Publishing House, circa 1860. From the Library of Congress Prints and Photographs Division, Washington, D.C.

On the back cover: First row (left to right): John Bakken's sod house in Milton, North Dakota; Oswego starch factory in Oswego, New York. Second row (left to right): *American Progress*, painted by John Gast in 1872; the Battle of Palo Alto. Third row (left to right): Pony Express rider pursued by Native Americans on the plains; Union soldiers investigating the rubble of a Southern building.

CONTENTS

INTRODUCTION

Think about how easy it is to stay in touch with your friends and family. You can write an e-mail or send an instant message and within seconds you can say hello to a friend. Or, you can dial your cell phone and tell your parents you'll be home late. If you send a Federal Express package to your cousin who lives ten states away, she'll have it the next day.

THE PONY EXPRESS CONNECTS THE COUNTRY

Now try to think back to a time when there were no computers, cell phones, airplanes, or trucks. How would you get your message through? Men and women who had made the long journey west to California to seek their fortunes in the gold rush in the 1850s faced this dilemma. They had given up everything, leaving their friends and families. Working hard day and night, they were lonely and tired. They wanted to let their families know that they were OK. They also longed for news from back home. In some cases, they wanted to send the exciting news that they had struck it rich. The problem was that there was no way to do any of these things quickly. A letter or package could take months to travel between California and the East Coast.

The Pony Express filled a need in the expanding United States of the nineteenth century. Western settlers homesick for their families and interested in news from the East needed faster, more reliable mail service. This 1862 map, created by John Calvin Smith, shows the Pony Express route stretching across the vast lands of the West. The Pony Express lasted for eighteen months, closing down as a result of the completion of the transcontinental telegraph.

In 1860, William Russell, Alexander Majors, and William Waddell proposed a plan to solve this problem. Their idea was to set up a system of horses and riders that would speed the mail between St. Joseph, Missouri, and San Francisco, California. Each rider on the route would travel about 40 miles (64 kilometers), changing horses every 10 to 12 miles (16 to 19 km). If all went as planned, the mail would make the 1,966-mile (3,164 km) trip in just ten days. They called their system the Pony Express.

Russell, Majors, and Waddell spent several months preparing for the first run of the Pony Express. On the afternoon of April 3, 1860, a horse and rider left each of the two cities at the ends of the route. Crowds in St. Joseph and San Francisco cheered as the mail was thrown over the saddle of the horse waiting to speed away. Many of the riders who made the first run faced stormy spring weather, mud, and dark nights. The first trip was a great success anyway. The mail reached each end of the route in just under ten days.

After the first successful ride, the Pony Express continued carrying the mail once a week. Later, the Pony Express began making the trip twice a week. People, especially in far-off California, were thrilled. Pony Express riders carried newspapers with important speeches, election results, and other news. Letters from friends and family arrived in weeks instead of months.

People liked the Pony Express not only because it brought news and letters. They were also impressed with the brave riders who carried the mail. The writer Mark Twain observed Pony Express riders when he made a trip across the West. He described the dedication of the riders in his 1872 book *Roughing It*:

> No matter what the time of day or night . . . and no matter whether it was winter or summer, raining, snowing, hailing, or sleeting, or whether his [route] was a level, straight road or a crazy trail over mountain crags and precipices, or whether it led through peaceful regions or regions that swarmed with hostile Indians, he must always be ready to leap into the saddle and be off like the wind.

Despite its success, the Pony Express did not last long. Just eighteen months after it began, the Pony Express stopped running. The telegraph, a method of sending messages quickly over a wire, finally connected the country from coast to coast in October 1861. Soon there was no more need for the Pony Express. Although many were sad to see it go, it has not been forgotten. Nearly 150 years later, the legend still lives on.

TIMELINE

1673 —— Mail begins traveling regularly between Boston and New York City.

1843 —— The Great Migration of 1843 becomes the first caravan to bring settlers across the entire 2,000 miles (3,129 km) of the Oregon Trail to the U.S. West.

January 24, 1848 —— Gold discovered at Sutter's Mill, California.

1849 —— The gold rush begins.

1856 —— Seventy-five thousand California residents sign a petition asking the U.S. government to start official mail to the West.

1857 —— The Butterfield Express Company begins carrying mail between Missouri and San Francisco; the mail takes twenty-three days to travel.

January 27, 1860 —— William Russell sends a telegram to his son, John, announcing his idea for the Pony Express.

TIMELINE

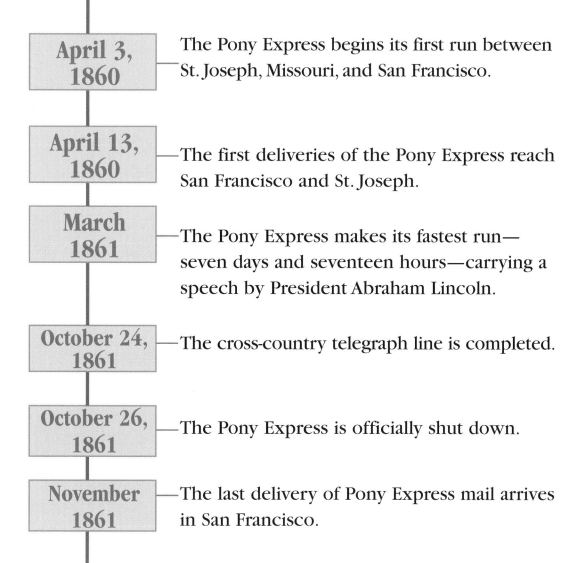

April 3, 1860	The Pony Express begins its first run between St. Joseph, Missouri, and San Francisco.
April 13, 1860	The first deliveries of the Pony Express reach San Francisco and St. Joseph.
March 1861	The Pony Express makes its fastest run—seven days and seventeen hours—carrying a speech by President Abraham Lincoln.
October 24, 1861	The cross-country telegraph line is completed.
October 26, 1861	The Pony Express is officially shut down.
November 1861	The last delivery of Pony Express mail arrives in San Francisco.

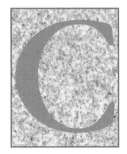

CHAPTER 1

BEFORE THE PONY EXPRESS

When America was first being settled, there was no formal mail system. Friends or neighbors would carry messages for each other if they happened to be traveling to other towns. Frustrated by the slow pace and unreliability of these methods, colonists were eager to find a better way.

By 1673, mail had begun traveling between Boston and New York City on a regular basis. The mail was not delivered directly to recipients. Instead, people picked up their letters at a central mail station. In the 1700s, the system was improved and mail traveled on stagecoaches. Special roads called post roads were created so the mail could get through easily. However, the system was still slow, and it was very expensive.

This milestone marks State Route 9, Boston Post Road, in Worcester County, Massachusetts. The stone reads, "56 Miles From Boston." Mail was easily delivered between the major East Coast cities of the early United States using special roads designated solely for postal travel. Boston Post Road was originally an Indian trail and eventually served as the main land connection between New York and Boston. In 1673, King Charles II declared it the first official mail route in North America.

The New West

By the middle of the 1800s, the mail system in the eastern United States was well developed. Mail traveled by stagecoaches or railroads, and people could even send telegrams for very fast service. However, something different was happening in the West. People had begun moving to the land that is now California and Oregon in the 1840s.

The journey west was very difficult. Some people sailed 13,000 miles (20,922 km) around the southern tip of South America to get to California. Others decided to take the Oregon Trail, a rough overland route that took them through the desert and mountains and Native American territories. There were many hardships and deaths along the way.

The high risks and costs in moving west kept many people in the eastern part of the country. But in 1848, gold was discovered in California. The prospect of finding riches in California drove many people to head west. So many people left the East that soon there were nearly half a million non-Native American people in California and Oregon. Most of them had left their families behind. They needed a way to communicate with people back home.

Getting the Mail to California

Early settlers in California and Oregon received their news and letters by boat. There was no regular system of mail. People in the East might simply hand a passenger a package and hope that they would deliver it when they reached the West. Men who were working in the gold mines or on their individual claims had no way of knowing if there was a letter waiting for them. And, of

The San Francisco post office was the only center for mail distribution on the West Coast when the Pony Express began. This lithograph by William Endicott and Co., circa 1850, shows the bustle of crowds waiting in line for their mail and newspapers. The arrival of mail brought about an excitement that was unmatched. As soon as the steamer carrying the mail was in sight, word traveled to the post office and on to the people, and soon the city was vibrating with anticipation of news from the East.

course, none of them wanted to leave their claims to go check. If they did, someone else might steal their spot.

A smart businessman named Alexander Todd had a solution. Todd traveled around the gold mines in California and Oregon collecting $1 from anyone who wanted him to check their mail in San Francisco. If any mail had arrived for his customer, he would bring it back, and the miner would pay him $16 in gold dust. This service was a huge success, and soon others were setting up similar systems. It worked well for everyone involved, especially the

THE WAY THEY GO TO CALIFORNIA.

This 1849 lithograph by Nathaniel Currier satirizes the rush to travel west in hopes of cashing in on California's riches. Entitled *The Way They Go to California,* the work shows men with picks and shovels, trying any method of transport that will get them to the West. In the foreground, men tumble into the water to gain passage on a ship, the least direct way to the West. The background images reflect the absurdity of the notion of air travel at the time. In the upper left corner, each passenger aboard Rufus Porter's so-called aerial locomotive (which was never built) is instructed to "provide a boy to hold his hair on."

miners, who were happy to have news from their families. Alonzo Delano, a writer visiting the California mines, described the arrival of the mail in his travel diary: "The [mail] has arrived! Every pick and shovel is dropped . . . and they crowd around the store [asking], 'Have you got a letter for me?' With what joy it is seized, and they care little whether they pay two or five dollars for it, they've got a letter."

These delivery systems worked well, but letters still took months to reach California. By 1856, 75,000 California residents had signed a petition to get the U.S. government to start an official mail service for the West. A year later, California got what it asked for. U.S. postmaster general Aaron Brown hired John Butterfield's stagecoach company to carry the mail to California. The route the mail would take was 2,800 miles (4,506 km) long. Starting from Missouri, the coaches would travel south to Texas and across the southwest to San Diego, California. The route then turned north to San Francisco and Oregon. The journey would take twenty-three days.

A New Idea

There was a problem with this plan, and many people were unhappy about it. The mail could have been transported on a route that was shorter and faster. That route would have gone through the North. The postmaster general was from Kentucky. Northerners accused Brown of playing favorites by picking a Southern route. Tensions between the North and South were building in the United States. The choice of this route only made things worse.

California had not yet chosen sides in the debate about slavery and civil war. It seemed to be leaning toward joining the North. Northerners wanted to make sure California stayed on their side, and they knew it was important for mail and news to reach California quickly. If the mail went through Southern states, there was a chance it would not even make it to California.

Several people believed there was a better and faster way to get mail to California. Historians aren't sure who came up with

Engraved by J.C.Buttre

Your Obt. servt.
Aaron V. Brown

Aaron Venable Brown (1795–1859) practiced law with future president James K. Polk before being elected to various political positions. He served as postmaster general from 1857 to 1859, during the Buchanan administration. Although Brown might have shown bias in choosing a Southern route for mail travel, he did make great advances in opening mail service to the West. This engraving of Brown is credited to J. C. Buttre and is housed in the Library of Congress.

the idea first. Most believe that William Gwin, a California senator, was riding his horse to Washington, D.C., with a man named B. F. Ficklin. On the way, they discussed the idea of using horses to speed the mail to California. Ficklin worked for a man named William Russell, who decided to make the idea work.

Russell and his partners, Alexander Majors and William Waddell, already had a successful shipping company. In 1850, they had 6,000 wagons and 75,000 oxen to pull them. Thousands of their employees helped ship food and supplies to people living in the West. Their wagons then brought gold, animal skins, and other goods back to the East.

On January 27, 1860, William Russell sent a telegram to his son, John, in Lexington, Missouri. It read: "Have determined to establish a Pony Express to Sacramento, California, commencing 3rd of April. Time ten days." Many people thought this idea was crazy. They said the route was too rough, with too many mountains. They warned him that the weather would make things difficult and that there were unfriendly Native Americans along the route. Even his partners didn't think it was a good idea. But Russell convinced them to set up the Pony Express anyway. He felt it was his duty to his country. He was strongly on the side of the North in the growing move to war. He wanted to make sure the mail got through to California quickly.

Soon after Russell sent the telegram to his son, word of the Pony Express spread. The Leavenworth, Kansas, *Daily Times* ran a headline on January 30, 1860, that stated, "Great Express Adventure from Leavenworth to Sacramento in Ten Days. Clear the Track and Let the Pony Come Through."

CHAPTER 2

PLANNING THE PONY EXPRESS

As the news about the idea for the Pony Express traveled across the country, people began to get very excited. This was especially true in California, as residents realized they might be able to get news from the East in about ten days—instead of the many months it was taking at the time.

Before the Pony Express could begin, there was plenty of work to do. Russell, Majors, and Waddell had to hire riders and buy horses. They also had to hire people to feed and take care of the horses and riders along the route. Stations where the riders and horses would live had to be built.

William Waddell *(top left)*, William Russell *(top right)*, and Alexander Majors *(bottom)* were the driving forces behind the Pony Express. Waddell (1807–1872) handled the money for the business. He and Russell (1812–1872), a successful businessman, hooked up with accomplished freighter Majors (1814–1900) to form a freighting company before starting the Pony Express. But their success was short-lived: The three never recovered from the financial disappointment of the Pony Express, and they died broken men.

Preparing the Route

Russell and his partners decided that the Pony Express would run between St. Joseph and San Francisco. The railroad and the telegraph lines from the East ended in St. Joseph, so that was a good place to start.

One of the first tasks for Russell, Majors, and Waddell was to get the 1,966-mile (3,164 km) route ready. The route was long and some of it went straight through mountains and deserts. They divided the route into five sections, each managed by a man in charge of supplying the stations. The manager would hire new riders if someone quit. Managers were also responsible for keeping the route in good shape.

To make this long journey in ten days or less, Pony Express horses would have to run 10 to 12 miles per hour (16 to 19 km/h). There would be no time for rest stops. Because riders would have to change horses often, stations were built 10 to 15 miles (16 to 24 km) apart. Riders could change horses at each station. Each rider would change horses four or five times and then would stop at a home station. There, a new rider would take over. The first rider would sleep, eat, and prepare for his next ride.

Some of the stations were difficult to get to or were far from towns and water supplies. It was hard to provide those stations with food and water. But Russell, Majors, and Waddell knew it was important to keep the horses and riders in good shape, so they built roads to make it easier to get to the stations. They did whatever it took and paid whatever was necessary to make sure the route was ready.

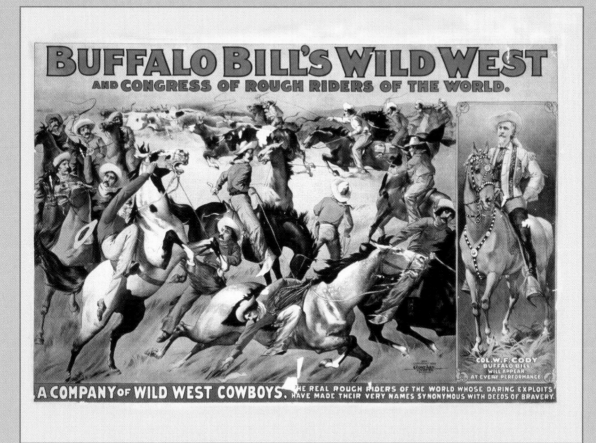

The partners in the Pony Express hired young, adventurous men to transport the mail to the West. One such rider was fifteen-year-old William F. Cody (1846–1917), later known as Buffalo Bill. Cody made the longest continuous ride (322 miles [518 km]) over dangerous parts of the trail in twenty-one hours and forty minutes using twenty-one horses. After the Pony Express ended, Cody created a wildly successful traveling entertainment show called Buffalo Bill's Wild West, which included a reenactment of the Pony Express.

Hiring the Riders and Buying the Horses

"Wanted: Young Skinny Wiry Fellows. Not Over Eighteen. Must Be Expert Riders Willing to Risk Death Daily. Orphans Preferred. Wages $25 per Week."

That was the ad that appeared in newspapers along the route the Pony Express would take. The ad caught the attention of many young men. They liked the idea of the salary (which was high for the time). Also, "most of the young fellows . . . were looking for something exciting, and the 'Pony' was just what they wanted," said Bill Cates, a rider interviewed by Arthur Chapman in his book *The Pony Express*.

One of the route managers placed an ad in the *Sacramento Union* in March 1860 looking for "ten or a dozen men familiar with the management of horses." Almost 200 men showed up to apply for the job of managing the stations and caring for the horses.

By the time the Pony Express began, eighty of the best riders had been hired. All of them had to sign a pledge that said they would not swear, drink liquor, or fight with any of the other employees in the company. They also had to agree to take good care of the horses. Many of the riders were young and had to be in good shape so they wouldn't get tired easily. All of them had to be skinny because the horses had to carry the lightest load possible.

As important as it was to hire good riders, it was even more important to get good horses. There was no way the Pony Express could keep to its strict schedule if it did not have the fastest, most reliable horses. Russell, Majors, and Waddell decided that they would need thoroughbred horses that could run fast over the plains in the eastern part of the route. For the mountain

Pony Express rider Frank Webner poses for this 1861 photograph while a Native American woman secures his *mochila* (mailbag). When they were hired, riders were required to take the following oath: "I do hereby swear . . . that I will, under no circumstances, use profane language, that I will drink no intoxicating liquors, that I will not quarrel or fight with any other employee of the firm, and that in every respect I will conduct myself honestly, be faithful to my duties, and so direct all my acts as to win the confidence of my employers, so help me God."

trails in the West, they would buy mustang horses that were used to running over rough roads.

They put ads in newspapers looking for good horses. They were willing to pay about $175 for each horse—a lot of money at the time. Soon they had 500 horses ready to go.

Preparing the Equipment

To keep up the fast pace, the horses would not be able to carry a heavy load. Heavy saddles or heavy riders would slow them down. The riders would use special lightweight saddles, with a mailbag called a *mochila* placed on top.

Mochilas fit over the saddle and could be fastened and taken off very easily. Each time the rider changed horses, he would take

PONY EXPRESS!

CHANGE OF
TIME!

REDUCED
RATES!

10 Days to San Francisco!

LETTERS

WILL BE RECEIVED AT THE

OFFICE, 84 BROADWAY,

NEW YORK,

Up to **4** P. M. every TUESDAY,

AND

Up to **2½** P. M. every SATURDAY,

Which will be forwarded to connect with the PONY EXPRESS leaving
ST. JOSEPH, Missouri,

Every WEDNESDAY and SATURDAY at 11 P. M.

TELEGRAMS

Sent to Fort Kearney on the mornings of MONDAY and FRIDAY, will connect with **PONY** leaving St. Joseph, WEDNESDAYS and SATURDAYS.

EXPRESS CHARGES.

LETTERS weighing half ounce or under..............$1 00
For every additional half ounce or fraction of an ounce 1 00
In all cases to be enclosed in 10 cent Government Stamped Envelopes,
And all Express CHARGES Pre-paid.

☞ PONY EXPRESS ENVELOPES For Sale at our Office.

WELLS, FARGO & CO., Ag'ts.

New York, Ju'y 1, 1861.

SLOTE & JANES, STATIONERS AND PRINTERS, 95 FULTON STREET, NEW YORK

Once preparations for the Pony Express were underway, advertisements for its services began to appear, stirring up excitement across the country. Not only did crowds of people gather to witness the launching of the first ride, but riders were frequently met with cheers at each town they reached. Indeed, the mere sound of the thunderous galloping of a horse's hooves was cause for great excitement in the towns along the route. See transcription on page 56.

the mochila off the saddle and throw it over the saddle of the new horse. This allowed riders to change horses very quickly. In fact, they changed so quickly that it usually took only fifteen seconds for a rider and his mochila to switch from one horse to another.

The mochila had four pouches for mail, two on either side. Each pouch—called a cantina—could be locked with a special key. At the beginning of each run, mail would be locked into three of the four cantinas. That mail could only be taken out in San Francisco, Salt Lake City, or St. Joseph. The fourth cantina was for any mail the rider picked up at stations along the way.

Even the mail itself had to be lightweight so the horses would not be overloaded. Letters and special editions of newspapers were printed on very thin paper. The mail was then wrapped in special silk that was coated in oil to repel water. This would protect the mail from rain, snow, and sweat from the riders and horses.

Final Preparations

By the end of March 1860, preparations were nearly complete. Russell, Majors, and Waddell had finished building 190 stations and had hired people to work at them. The riders and horses were ready.

On March 26, 1860, notices announcing the Pony Express were put in the *New York Herald* and the *St. Louis Republic*: "To San Francisco in 8 days. The first courier of the Pony Express will leave the Missouri River on Tuesday April 3rd at 5 o'clock PM and will run regularly weekly hereafter, carrying a letter mail only." The announcement also gave directions for where to take mail so that it could be included in the first run.

CHAPTER 3

AND THEY'RE OFF!

Everything was in place. Letters from all over the East Coast were on their way to St. Joseph. In San Francisco, people gathered their own news and letters in preparation for the trip east. Riders waited eagerly at each end of the route for the moment when they would be able to begin their historic journey.

Late in the afternoon of April 3, 1860, crowds began gathering in St. Joseph to celebrate the beginning of the first Pony Express run. A brass band played, and Mayor M. Jeff Thompson was ready to make a speech. There was just one problem: the train carrying the mail from New York had not arrived. It had missed a connection in Detroit and would be three hours late.

People tried to be patient. They listened to Mayor Thompson explain how the train would soon run all the way to the West Coast. Railroad companies were working on extending the railroads from Missouri to San Francisco, but the job would not be complete for another two years. Until then, the Pony Express would connect the country. According to Arthur Chapman, the mayor asked the crowd to "give three cheers for the Pony Express, three cheers for the first overland passage of the United States Mail!"

ST. JOSEPH DAILY GAZETTE.

PONY EXPRESS EDITION.

ST. JOSEPHh, Mo., APRIL 3rd,—6 O'CLOCK, P. M.

The *St. Joseph Daily Gazette* printed a special Pony Express Edition on light-weight paper for the riders to carry west. The first edition, dated April 3, 1860, is shown above. It was carried in the mochila of the first express ride to California, along with eighty-four other pieces of mail. This edition is displayed in the California State Library. See transcription excerpt on pages 56 and 57.

The first rider and his horse waited to begin. Some people in the crowd were so excited that they began plucking hair out of the tail of the horse to keep as a souvenir. To protect the horse, the rider brought it back to the stable until the run began.

Soon the train arrived from New York. Forty-nine letters, six telegrams, and special editions of newspapers from the East were locked in the cantinas. The mochila was thrown over the saddle. A cannon was fired, and the first Pony Express rider

One of the most exciting and important pieces of mail to travel by Pony Express was news of Abraham Lincoln's election *(above)*. This report was written on the outside of a letter sent to the *Rocky Mountain News* in Denver, postmarked November 8, 1860. The upper left corner of the letter reads, "Election News. Lincoln Elected."

was off! The next day, the *St. Joseph Weekly West* described the departure:

> The Missouri and Pacific United!
> The Greatest Enterprise of Modern Times!!
> At a quarter past seven o'clock last evening . . . horse and rider started off amid the loud and continuous cheers of the [crowd], all anxious to witness . . . [this great] enterprise.

The First Trip West

Historians don't agree on the name of the first rider to leave St. Joseph. Some think it was a man named Bill Richardson. Others think it was Johnny Frye. There is no way to know for sure because none of the records of Russell, Majors, and Waddell's company remain. Also, many of the St. Joseph newspapers from the time were destroyed during riots at the start of the Civil War.

Whoever the first rider was, he and his horse dashed off to the ferry that took them across the Missouri River to Elwood, Kansas. Once they reached the other side of the river, they raced off. They were trying to make up the time they had lost because of the late train. The rider rushed from station to station, changing his horse at each one. Finally he reached his home station, where he turned the mochila over to a new rider. He had ridden 80 miles (129 km) in just six hours and twenty-five minutes. Even though it had been dark the whole way, he had made up some of the lost time and the Pony Express was almost on schedule again.

Jim Beatley, the next rider, took over in Seneca, Kansas, and continued riding through the dark night to Rock Creek, Nebraska. The next few riders raced through the next day and night, making up time whenever they could. By the time eighteen-year-old Bill Campbell took over the mochila in Fort Kearney, Nebraska, it was beginning to rain hard. He and the next riders battled a strong storm, with high winds and driving rain. This slowed them down, and the Pony Express began to fall behind schedule.

When Bart Riles took over in Fort Churchill, Nevada, the storm was over. He was heading into the desert, though, and faced danger from the Paiute Indians. To avoid the Paiute, he had

This engraving by Frederic Remington, from around 1895, depicts a Pony Express rider changing mounts at a station. Riders had only two minutes to change horses when they reached a station. As they approached, they loosened the mochila and threw it ahead to the station keeper, who would then fasten it on a new horse. The keeper would have saddled and prepared the new horse ahead of time so that it would be ready to go when the rider charged into the station.

to take a long detour and lost more time. The next few riders raced through the desert of Nevada and the mountains of Utah.

Eventually, the first rider reached Salt Lake City. On April 11, the *Salt Lake City Deseret News* wrote about the arrival of the rider: "[Salt Lake City] is now within six days' communication with the frontier [Missouri] . . . a result which we Utahians, accustomed to receive news three months after date, can well appreciate."

The Pony Express run continued through more rain, mud, and mountains. Thomas King, the rider who took over the run in Echo Canyon, Utah, started off well. Then another storm began, and the trail grew slippery. King's horse fell, throwing King off and sending the mochila flying over a cliff. King had to waste precious time finding the mochila. As soon as he did, he threw it back over the saddle and continued the run. Amazingly, he made it to the next station on time.

The race continued across Nevada and into California. On the afternoon of April 13, Bill Hamilton reached Placerville, California. The next day, the *Placerville Union* described his arrival: "The reception of the Pony Express here was most enthusiastic. Flags were suspended, bands of music played, and the entire populace cheering. Our Mayor . . . escorted the rider . . . into and out of the city."

The people of Sacramento were even more excited. The April 14 issue of the *Sacramento Union* described how the crowds waited for the rider to appear until "the pony was seen coming at a rattling pace down . . . the street . . . which was wild with excitement. [The mail arrived] in ten days from St. Joseph to Sacramento. Hip, hip, hurrah for the Pony Carrier!"

From Sacramento, the last rider boarded the steamship that would take him down the river to San Francisco. Finally, around midnight, the Pony Express arrived at the last stop: San Francisco. The riders had accomplished exactly what had been promised. They had made the 1,966-mile (3,164 km) ride in just less than ten days. The first westward run was a success.

The Pony Leaves San Francisco

At about the same time the first horse was leaving St. Joseph, the first eastward rider was getting a big send-off in San Francisco. Crowds filled the streets and bands played as the first rider prepared for his ride. At 4:00 PM, he and his horse headed out of San

Pony Express rider Warren Upson is depicted battling a fierce snowstorm in the Sierra Nevada in this image. One of the obstacles faced by Pony Express riders was extreme weather, which not only slowed down the rides but also posed great danger to the lives of the men and their horses. Because it was so difficult for the horses to get through the deep snow, mules were used to pack down the trails.

Francisco and stepped aboard the steamship that would take them up the river to Sacramento. The official ride would not really begin until they reached Sacramento (about 85 miles [137 km] away). After this first run, the riders of the regular route would end and begin their route in Sacramento. The mail would then be put on a steamship to travel the river between the two cities.

When the rider arrived in Sacramento at about 2:00 AM, it was pouring rain. A new rider, Sam Hamilton, grabbed the mochila and sped away through the rain. The mud and dark night slowed the horse down, but Hamilton did his best to keep the Pony Express on schedule. It got harder to keep to the schedule as they began climbing higher into the Sierra Nevada mountains. There, it was colder, and the trail was icy. Finally, Hamilton reached his home station of Sportsman's Hall and turned the mochila over to the new rider, Warren "Boston" Upson.

Upson had an even more difficult route ahead. He had to ride through steep, snow-covered mountains. The trails through the mountains had been filled with snow for days. Upson pushed on through the deep snowbanks, battling heavy winds. One of his horses got stuck in a snowbank. Another almost got swept away as they crossed the flooded American River. Somehow Upson managed to ride his 55-mile (89 km) route in just eight hours.

The next rider to take the mochila was "Pony Bob" Haslam. He was cheered on by miners in Carson City, Nevada. He arrived at his home station of Fort Churchill, Nevada, ahead of schedule. The first three riders had ridden 185 difficult miles (298 km) in fifteen hours and twenty minutes. The Pony Express was now nine hours ahead of schedule.

Over the next few days, the riders were not able to keep up this fast pace. They continued to battle bad weather. Wind, heavy

San Francisco celebrates the completion of the first Pony Express ride, as the last in the chain of riders from St. Joseph arrives just before midnight on April 13, 1860. Throughout the rest of the Pony Express's run, the horses rode only as far as Sacramento, where the mail was loaded on a boat and carried to San Francisco.

rain, and thick mud slowed them down. Nevertheless, the riders did their best, and the last rider arrived in St. Joseph almost exactly ten days after the first had left San Francisco. The first run had been an amazing success. Now everyone wanted to know if the Pony Express could continue to run on schedule, week after week.

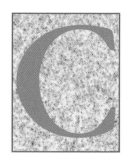

CHAPTER 4

Excitement about the Pony Express continued to build after the first successful run. People in the western states were especially happy. In the past, it had taken months to get news. It seemed like a miracle to hear about events in the East just ten days after they happened.

THE WEEKLY RIDE

People in the East were excited, too. Newspapers were now able to write stories with current news from the West. Some newspapers in big cities hired writers to work in St. Joseph. These reporters would wait for news to come in on the Pony Express. As soon as it did, they would write stories and send them by telegraph to the newspapers. Their stories would carry the headline "By Pony Express."

People weren't just excited about the Pony Express because it brought news. They were also interested in the brave men who made the Pony Express happen. Every day the riders faced challenges from the weather and Native Americans. The *Kansas City Western Journal of Commerce* printed a story about the Pony Express on August 9, 1860. The story described the excitement of the ride:

[A]way flies the Express pony with news of all the nations ... on his back ... [The riders] must hurry on through every danger and difficulty, and bring the Atlantic and Pacific shores within a week of each other. No stop, no stay, no turning aside for rest, shelter, or safety, but right forward. By sun-light, and moon-light, and starlight, and through the darkness of the midnight storms, he must fly on and on toward the distant goal.

The writer Mark Twain saw a Pony Express rider while he was on a trip across Nevada. He described the experience in his book *Roughing It*:

[A]cross the endless . . . prairie a black speck appears against the sky . . . In a second or two it becomes a horse and rider, rising and falling . . . nearer and nearer still, and the flutter of the hoofs comes faintly to the ear—another instant and . . . man and horse . . . go swinging away like the belated fragment of a storm.

The Riders

Many people considered the Pony Express riders to be heroes. The riders did whatever it took to get the mail through to the next station safely and on time. The riders knew they were doing exciting and important work, but they didn't give much thought to that. They were too busy just getting the mail through. Billy Fisher, a rider interviewed by Arthur Chapman in his book about the Pony Express, said, "It was all exciting, only we didn't think much about it that way. We just took things as they came; it was all in a day's work."

Johnny Frye (1840–1863) is often given credit for being the first Pony Express rider to leave St. Joseph. Barely out of his teens, and weighing less than 120 pounds (54 kilograms), Frye became one of the most famous riders to hit the westward trail. His speed averaged 12.5 miles per hour (20 km/h), including station stops. Girls who lived near Frye's route gathered to watch the young man gallop through town, desperate to catch glimpses of him and to feed him cakes and bits of fried dough. To help Frye grip these treats as he raced by, they cut holes in the centers, creating— legend has it—the very first doughnuts.

The riders had to know how to deal with the weather and with the land they would be riding over. They had to be excellent horseback riders who were used to being in the saddle for hours at a time. Riders couldn't be scared of anything, and they had to be well behaved.

William F. "Billy" Fisher (1839–1919) is another well-known rider of the Pony Express. Twenty years old when he started, his route went through eastern Nevada and later through Utah. During the Paiute Indian War, Fisher rode 300 miles (483 km) in thirty hours to warn station keepers that the Paiute were destroying stations in the area. After the Pony Express closed down, Fisher explored many careers, working as a rancher, lawyer, and tooth extractor.

Riding for the Pony Express was difficult and tiring work. Bill Campbell, another Pony Express rider, told Arthur Chapman that he was very excited to be hired. However, he was

soon to find that 'riding express' had more hard work than fun in it. We got exciting adventures at times to help keep things . . . interesting . . . but our work was strenuous. It took sheer grit and endurance at times to carry the mail through.

Not many riders worked for the Pony Express for all of the eighteen months it ran. Many quit, especially during the cold winter months. Jack Keetley was one of the few riders who did work for the Pony Express the whole time it was operating.

Keetley once rode thirty-one hours straight, covering 341 miles (549 km). During that ride, he fell asleep in the saddle. Luckily, his horse continued on to the station with Keetley slouched over the mochila.

One of the most important runs the riders made was in March 1861. President Abraham Lincoln had just been elected, and he made his inaugural address about the conflict between the Union and the Confederacy. (The Confederacy—a group of Southern states that practiced slavery—wanted to break away from the United States. They were willing to fight a war to do so. The Northern states—known as the Union—wanted to abolish slavery and keep the country together.) The Northern states felt that it was important that the speech reach California quickly. They hoped the speech would help convince Californians to support their cause and lend their support. The Union would need troops and money if there was to be a war with the Confederacy.

To get the speech to California as quickly as possible, extra riders and horses were added to the route. The run turned out to be the fastest in the history of the Pony Express. The mail reached San Francisco in seven days and seventeen hours. George Washington "Wash" Perkins was one of the riders who helped deliver Lincoln's speech. He described the situation to Arthur Chapman in *The Pony Express:*

> Our orders were to get the mail through no matter what . . . You see, the West was all in excitement over the coming war. There were men of Northern and Southern sympathy on the frontier. It was a grave question which side California and the other parts of the West would take.

A page from a draft of Abraham Lincoln's first inaugural address, delivered on March 4, 1861. This address, so important to the pre–Civil War relations between the North and South, was eagerly anticipated by Western settlers, who received it by Pony Express. Lincoln specifically changed the tone from earlier drafts to a softer, more impassioned plea for the two sides to come together: "We must not be enemies. Though passion may have strained, it must not break our bonds of affection." See transcription excerpt on page 57.

Bill Campbell also helped carry Lincoln's speech on that important ride. In April 1861, he carried the news of the attack on Fort Sumter, South Carolina, the first battle of the Civil War. He told Arthur Chapman, "such things broke the routine, and made every Pony Express rider feel that he was helping make history."

The Horses

Riding for the Pony Express was not easy, but many riders say that good horses certainly made things easier. Bill Campbell told Arthur Chapman, "One thing that did help was our horses. I always was given good ones to ride . . . It was a joy to ride these intelligent animals." The horses were as dedicated as the riders. During one run, Paiute Indians shot a Pony Express horse with two arrows. He finished the run anyway. By the time the wounded horse arrived at the station, his light-colored hair was covered in blood and dust and he looked nearly black. After that, his nickname was Black Billy.

Many of the horses knew their routes so well that they would continue on the route even if something happened to the rider. Thomas Owen King, another Pony Express rider, described to Arthur Chapman how dedicated his horses were: "Many a time I went to sleep in the saddle, and the pony would keep up his pace . . . The ponies, when they knew what was expected of them, would keep up the pace from one end of a run to the other."

About seventy-five horses were needed to make one run from East to West. They were the best horses money could buy. Some of the mustangs acquired for the western end of the route had been rounded up off the prairies and mountains. These horses were not very tame, but they were very intelligent and were good at running through the rocky mountains and canyons.

This photograph, taken by William Henry Jackson and housed in the Harold B. Lee Library at Brigham Young University, shows a Pony Express station and the landscape surrounding a portion of the route. While riders had to contend with treacherous weather conditions and dangerous Indian wars, they also faced endless stretches of barren wilderness. Station keepers were just as lonely, living in isolation and waiting for the brief excitement of riders arriving to change mounts.

Life at the Stations

The people who worked at the Pony Express stations were chosen as carefully as the riders and the horses. Life at the stations was not easy. Most were miles from the nearest town. Station workers saw very few people other than the riders.

Some of the stations were very small. These were called relay or swing stations. At these stations, riders just switched horses. Usually there were two men who worked there. One man cared for the horses and the other took care of the station. These stations were not fancy. Most had dirt floors and no real furniture. Many relay station keepers slept on the floor, using animal skins as blankets. Some of the stations were just dug out of a hillside. Others were simple shacks made from whatever material was handy. Larger stations, where riders lived, were called home stations. More horses lived at these stations, and several people worked there. Home station houses were larger, and the conditions were a little better.

Food at the stations was not fancy. Sometimes riders and station keepers had fresh meat from animals they were able to kill. Most of the time they just had bread, dried beans, dried fruit, and coffee. It was difficult to get supplies to the stations. Russell, Majors, and Waddell shipped supplies in wagons to the home stations, which were then shipped to the relay stations. Sometimes shipments were delayed and the station keepers had to make do with whatever supplies they had left. At some stations, managers could grow hay to feed the horses. This was not possible in the desert, so those stations depended on the shipments from the home stations.

Bill Streeper supplied the stations out in the desert near Salt Lake City. He told Arthur Chapman:

> It wasn't easy . . . to keep the stations along the line supplied with hay and grain and food . . . [T]here were no roads to speak of built when the Pony Express was started. We couldn't haul very big loads. If we tried to carry too much in our squeaky wagons we might break down in the desert miles from water.

Life at the stations was sometimes lonely and difficult. The difficulties and danger the riders faced on the Pony Express route were much more significant.

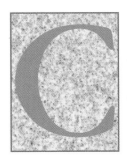

CHAPTER 5

Getting the mail through on time was hard enough. But there were many things that made the task nearly impossible. Certain parts of the Pony Express route were physically treacherous. The 500 miles (805 km) between Salt Lake City and Sacramento were probably the worst part. Included in that stretch were a few hundred miles of hot, dusty desert. The desert around Salt Lake City was particularly bad. This was because the sand was made up of alkali, a salty substance. Alkali produced thick, chalky dust that made it difficult for riders and horses to breathe. West of the deserts of Utah and Nevada, the riders had to face the Sierra Nevada. There challenges included steep trails, deep canyons, and blinding snowstorms.

HARDSHIPS ON THE TRAIL

Weather, especially during the winter months, made things hard on the riders and the horses. It was not easy to predict what a rider might face on any given ride. Heavy rains in the spring made the trails slippery with mud. Summer brought heat and dusty, dry conditions across the plains and deserts. Winter was the most difficult season. Snow piled up along the trail, and cold temperatures slowed the riders down.

Edward Martin photographed this scene of Salt Lake Valley, at the mouth of Echo Canyon, in the 1860s. This image illustrates the various types of terrain—from the dusty plains to rocky mountains—that Pony Express riders encountered on their journeys. The station shown in the photograph is Weber Station, built in 1853, which included a saloon, hotel, mail station, general store, jail, and Pony Express station.

Bill Campbell described one winter ride to Arthur Chapman in *The Pony Express.* During this ride, "The snow was from two to three feet deep along the Platte [River], with the temperature down to zero. It was impossible to make more than five miles an hour. Often I had to get off and lead my horse." It took Campbell twenty-four hours to make that particular run. This was partly because of the snow and partly because the rider wasn't waiting for him at the next station. Campbell had to ride 20 extra miles (32 km) through the blinding snow because he knew the mail had to get through.

Another storm caused rider Erasmus Egan's horse to slip and break its neck. Egan had to leave the horse behind and get the mail to the next station. He grabbed the mochila and began the 5-mile (8 km) walk to the next stop.

The Paiute Indian War

The Oregon Trail and the gold rush brought many white settlers to areas of the West where Native Americans had lived peacefully for years. The new settlers were not always respectful of the Native Americans' land or way of life. They killed animals the Native Americans depended on for food. In the area that is now Nevada and Utah, white settlers sometimes attacked the approximately 7,000 Paiute Indians who lived there.

By the time the Pony Express began, the problems between the settlers and the Paiute were getting worse. In addition, the winter the Pony Express began operating was a particularly bad one. Strong, heavy storms hit much of Nevada where the Paiute lived. The Paiute believed that the spirits that controlled the weather were angry because of all the white settlers who had moved to Nevada. A month after the Pony Express began, the Paiute met for a tribal council. Their chief, Winnemucca, hoped to avoid war. However, while the council was meeting, some Paiute attacked a Pony Express station. The station was burned and several men were killed. Winnemucca knew that the white settlers would attack and it would be very difficult to avoid a war.

Soon other Pony Express stations were being attacked. Seven stations were burned and several men—including one rider—were killed. More than 100 horses were stolen or killed. Riders faced danger on every route. Eventually, the danger grew so great that the mail had to be held near Salt Lake City. According to Roy

Paiute chief Winnemucca posed for this photograph around 1880. The Paiute were known for befriending white settlers. Winnemucca's father, also a chief, led white explorer Captain John Fremont to safety in California, a deed that was never forgotten. Winnemucca's daughter, known as Sarah, was very influential in the Paiute community. When her people fought against the spread of white settlers, she acted as an interpreter between the two warring parties and later became an activist for the plight of the Paiute.

Bloss's book, *Pony Express*, William Finney, the manager of the Pony Express in Carson City, Nevada, wrote to businessmen in Sacramento for help. He asked, "Will Sacramento help the Pony in its difficulty? We have [done a lot], have asked but little, and perhaps the people will assist."

Finney used the money he raised to buy supplies for the stations that had lost food, men, and horses in the Paiute attacks. He and several other men left Carson City on June 9, 1860. They dropped off supplies along the route, and a week later they arrived in Roberts Creek, Nevada, where 300 pieces of mail were waiting. A large group of U.S. soldiers escorted them back to

Although the presence of Indians was often a real threat to Pony Express riders, in truth, only one rider was ever captured, thanks to the high quality of the horses used by the Pony Express. These superior animals were often able to outrun horses ridden by Native Americans. During the Paiute Indian War, Pony Express stations were specially targeted for attack, resulting in the death of many employees and the theft of 150 horses.

Carson City with the mail. From there, mail continued along the regular route to San Francisco. When it arrived on June 25, it was the first time mail had gotten through in three months.

Eventually the Paiute stopped attacking the Pony Express stations. The Paiute Indian War had slowed down service, but it never stopped it completely. However, the war came with a price. Russell, Majors, and Waddell had to spend nearly $75,000 to rebuild and resupply all the stations that had been destroyed.

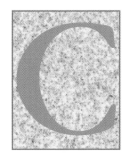CHAPTER 6

In many ways, the Pony Express was a great success. Mail ran regularly despite many difficulties. However, in one important way the Pony Express was a huge failure: it wasn't making money.

It was very expensive to send a letter by Pony Express. Not everyone could afford it. Customers paid $2 to $10 to send a letter. This was an extremely high price in the 1860s. Despite the high price, many people used the Pony Express. The problem was that it cost Russell, Majors, and Waddell almost $38 to carry each letter. They had to spend money on food for the horses and riders. Station masters and riders had to be paid. The company was spending about $25,000 a month to keep the Pony Express running. It's likely that the Pony Express never would have made money, no matter how many letters people sent.

THE END OF THE RIDE

Russell, Majors, and Waddell were not too concerned about the fact that the company was losing money. They thought the government would step in and help out. It was clear that the Pony Express was successfully carrying the mail. Not even problems like the Paiute attacks had stopped the mail. They were sure the government would be willing to make the Pony Express the official carrier of U.S. mail.

The government, however, had other ideas. The Butterfield Company was still the official carrier of U.S. mail. Butterfield carried the mail by stagecoach, and it still took about three weeks to reach California.

Russell finally decided to go to the government for help. He talked to John B. Floyd, the secretary of war. Floyd sent Russell to Godard Bailey, a man who managed bonds that belonged to Native Americans. The U.S. government had paid for Native American lands with these bonds. Instead of giving them the cash, the government was managing the money for the Native Americans. Bailey gave some of the bonds to Russell to help keep the Pony Express running. The problem was that this was illegal. The bonds did not belong to Bailey, and he had no right to give them away. Soon this deal was discovered and Russell was arrested.

The financial problems and the scandal involving Russell finally led to the breakup of Russell, Majors, and Waddell in January 1861. Although it was a big disappointment for the men who had formed the company, one good thing happened: the government did step in to help the Pony Express. New companies began managing the route, with help from the government. So the Pony Express ran on.

Competition from the Telegraph

The Pony Express was not to run for much longer, though. As fast as the horses and riders were, the telegraph was faster. The telegraph was an important communication device in the eastern United States. Telegraph machines quickly sent coded messages, called telegrams, through wires. However, the telegraph wires went only as far as Missouri, so the rest of the country was not able to use this device.

A Pony Express rider waves to men putting up telegraph poles on the prairie, in this wood engraving. The completion of the transcontinental telegraph line brought about the end of the Pony Express, as messages could be relayed much faster. The first message on the telegraph line was sent from Overland Telegraph Company president Horace W. Carpentier to President Abraham Lincoln. It read: "I announce to you that the telegraph to California has this day been completed. May it be a bond of perpetuity between the states of the Atlantic and those of the Pacific."

When the Civil War broke out in April 1861, it was more important than ever to get news to the West Coast quickly. Congress had already decided to investigate the possibility of extending the telegraph lines west from St. Joseph to California. They hired a man named Edward Creighton to do the job. He traveled west from St. Joseph on a mule to inspect the route. Creighton decided it would be possible to string the wires needed to carry telegraph messages.

When Congress heard that it would be possible, it offered a $40,000-a-year contract to any company willing to do the work. Western Union got the contract, and in July 1861 it began putting up the telegraph poles and wires. Work began from the

East and from the West at the same time. It became a contest between the two teams doing the work. Who would reach the midpoint—Salt Lake City—first?

As work began, the Pony Express continued carrying the mail between St. Joseph and Sacramento. Riders would let the telegraph crews know how far the other team had gotten. The team that had begun in St. Joseph reached Salt Lake City first—on October 20, 1861. The team working from the West arrived a few days later. On October 24, the line was complete. Messages could now be sent coast to coast in minutes instead of weeks. The Pony Express was about to go out of business.

The Pony Express Shuts Down

On October 26, 1861, the Pony Express was officially shut down. The mail runs that were underway at the time continued, so some mail was delivered in November.

In the eighteen months the Pony Express had been in business, 34,753 pieces of mail were delivered. The brave riders and horses had ridden 600,000 miles (965,606 km)—a distance equal to traveling around the globe twenty-four times. However, the Pony Express had never made any money. In fact, it may have lost between $100,000 and $500,000. With the telegraph in operation, there was no way for the Pony Express to compete.

Although people were excited about the telegraph, they were also disappointed that the Pony Express had been shut down. The *California Pacific* published a story about the end of the Pony Express, which said, "A fast and faithful friend has the Pony been to our far-off state. Summer and winter, storm and shine, day and night, he has traveled . . . back and forth till now his work is done. Good-bye Pony! . . . You have served us well."

NOTICE.

BY ORDERS FROM THE EAST,

THE PONY EXPRESS

WILL be DISCONTINUED.

The Last Pony coming this way left Atchinson, Kansas, yesterday.

oc·25-1t   WELLS, FARGO & CO., Agents.

The above announcement signaled the end of the Pony Express. The notice was printed in the October 26, 1861, issue of the *San Francisco Evening Bulletin*, but the last Pony Express delivery didn't reach San Francisco until the following month. Although it was a financial disaster, the Pony Express made great strides in mail delivery in the United States.

People in California were especially disappointed about the end of the Pony Express. They had come to depend on the Pony Express for easy communication with friends and family and businesspeople in the East. The telegraph was certainly a quicker way of sending and receiving messages. However, in the beginning the telegraph was not always reliable. There were delays, and it was quite expensive to send a message. The state government in California tried to get Congress to keep the Pony Express running, but Congress didn't think this was a worthwhile idea.

This 1960 postage stamp commemorating the 100th anniversary of the first Pony Express ride shows that the legend lived on, as it continues to do today. In addition to being the subject of stories, songs, and movies, the Pony Express is often regarded as a symbol of the Wild West. The excitement, courage, and danger involved in this endeavor were most certainly in keeping with the spirit of the growth of the United States as a nation.

When the Pony Express shut down, the horses were sold or used by other parts of the Overland Mail Company. Riders returned to their old jobs. Some became miners or worked on the railroad. Others became storekeepers or stagecoach drivers. One rider, John Fisher, became a mayor. Several riders went off to fight in the Civil War. The famous rider Johnny Frye was killed in a Civil War battle in Kansas.

The Pony Express Rides into History

Even though the Pony Express never made any money, it was a success in every other way. It connected the far-off West Coast with the rest of the country. Weather, rough country, and the threat of war slowed it down but never stopped it. The mail got through no matter what.

The historians Raymond and Mary Settle describe the successes of the Pony Express in their book *Saddles and Spurs*:

When difficulties and distance are taken into consideration, no better job was ever done in the history of the United States mail service. The men who planned and supervised it, and the youths who rode the lonely route day and night, in fair weather and foul, in peace or in war, deserve the highest praise.

People today continue to be fascinated with the Pony Express. On the 100th anniversary of the beginning of the Pony Express, there were several celebrations. There was also a reenactment ride of the Pony Express route. Riders left St. Joseph and Sacramento on July 19, 1960. They finished the ride in the same amount of time that the Pony Express had taken one hundred years earlier.

Once a year in Arizona, riders travel the 200 miles (322 km) between Holbrook and Scottsdale, carrying around 20,000 first-class letters for the U.S. Postal Service. This ride—and others like it—celebrates the legacy of the Pony Express.

Even though the Pony Express ran for just eighteen months, the horses, riders, and others who made it happen still live on. Books, movies, and television shows have depicted the bravery of the riders. The Pony Express has become a symbol of the strength and resourcefulness of the people who helped create the American West.

PRIMARY SOURCE TRANSCRIPTIONS

Page 24 Pony Express Poster

TRANSCRIPTION

Pony Express! Change of time! Reduced rates! Ten days to San Francisco! Letters will be received at the office, 84 Broadway, New York, up to 4PM every Tuesday, and up to 21/2 PM every Saturday, which will be forwarded to connect with the Pony Express leaving St. Joseph, Missouri, every Wednesday and Saturday at 11PM. Telegrams sent to Fort on the mornings of Monday and Friday will connect with Pony leaving St. Joseph, Wednesdays and Saturdays. Express charges. Letters weighing half ounce or under $1. For every additional half ounce or fraction of an ounce $1. In all cases to be enclosed in 10 cent government stamped envelopes, and all Express charges pre-paid. Pony Express envelopes for sale at our office. Wells, Fargo & Co., [Agents]. New York, July 1, 1861.

Page 27 *St. Joseph Daily Gazette*

TRANSCRIPTION EXCERPT
ST. JOSEPH DAILY GAZETTE
PONY EXPRESS EDITION
ST. JOSEPH, Mo., APRIL 3rd,—6 O'CLOCK, PM.
JOSEPH, MO.
[???]DAY, APRIL 8, 1860—5 PM.

Through the politeness of the Express Company, we are permitted to forward, by the first Pony Express, the first and only newspaper which goes out, and which will be the first paper ever transmitted from Missouri to California in eight days. The nature of the conveyance necessarily precludes our making up an edition of any considerable weight. It, however, contains a summary of the latest news received here by telegraph for some days past from all parts of the Union. We send it greeting to our brethren of the press of California.

The Pony Express Starts Today
Mr. W. H. Russell, the President of the Central Overland California and Pike's Peak Express Company, and Mr. Majors, a Director in the Company, arrived in this city yesterday morning, to be present this afternoon to witness the starting of the first pony from the office of the Company. The fame of these gentlemen for intelligent enterprise is as wide as the West, and is now about to be associated with a movement which will extend it from one ocean to the other.

The first pony will start this afternoon at 5 P.M., precisely. Letters will be received for all points up to 4:30 PM.

A special train will be run over the Hannibal & St. Joseph Railroad for the purpose of bringing the through messenger from New York.

The following is the Time Table which has been adopted. From this city to

Maryvill	12 hours
Fort Kearney	34"
Laramie	80"
Camp Floyd	128"
Carson City	188"
Placerville	226"
Sacramento	232"
San Francisco	240"

The second Carrier will leave St. Joseph Friday, the 13th, at 9 AM.

Page 40 Draft of Lincoln's First Inaugural Address

TRANSCRIPTION EXCERPT
First Inaugural Address
March 4, 1861

Fellow citizens of the United States: in compliance with a custom as old as the government itself, I appear before you to address you briefly and to take, in your presence, the oath prescribed by the Constitution of the United States, to be taken by the President "before he enters on the execution of his office."

One section of our country believes slavery is RIGHT, and ought to be extended, while the other believes it is WRONG, and ought not to be extended. This is the only substantial dispute. The fugitive-slave clause of the Constitution, and the law for the suppression of the foreign slave-trade, are each as well enforced, perhaps, as any law can ever be in a community where the moral sense of the people imperfectly supports the law itself. The great body of the people abide by the dry legal obligation in both cases, and a few break over in each. This, I think, cannot be perfectly cured; and it would be worse in both cases AFTER the separation of the sections than BEFORE. The foreign slave-trade, now imperfectly suppressed, would be ultimately revived, without restriction, in one section, while fugitive slaves, now only partially surrendered, would not be surrendered at all by the other.

Physically speaking, we cannot separate. We cannot remove our respective sections from each other, nor build an impassable wall between them. A husband and wife may be divorced, and go out of the presence and beyond the reach of each other; but the different parts of our country cannot do this. They cannot but remain face to face, and intercourse, either amicable or hostile, must continue between them. Is it possible, then, to make that intercourse more advantageous or more satisfactory after separation than before? Can aliens make treaties easier than friends can make laws? Can treaties be more faithfully enforced between aliens than laws can among friends? Suppose you go to war, you cannot fight always; and when, after much loss on both sides, and no gain on either, you cease fighting, the identical old questions as to terms of intercourse are again upon you.

In YOUR hands, my dissatisfied fellow-countrymen, and not in MINE, is the momentous issue of civil war. The government will not assail YOU. You can have no conflict without being yourselves the aggressors. YOU have no oath registered in heaven to destroy the government, while I shall have the most solemn one to "preserve, protect, and defend it."

I am loathe to close. We are not enemies, but friends. We must not be enemies. Though passion may have strained, it must not break our bonds of affection. The mystic chords of memory, stretching from every battlefield and patriot grave to every living heart and hearthstone all over this broad land, will yet swell the chorus of the Union when again touched, as surely they will be, by the better angels of our nature.

GLOSSARY

accustomed   Being used to something.

alkali   A salty substance present in the sand or soil in some dry areas.

bond   A certificate that states a promise to repay a debt at a certain time.

cantina   A pouch that holds mail on a mochila.

Confederacy   The eleven Southern states that decided to leave the United States in 1861.

council   A group that meets to decide an important issue.

crag   A steep cliff.

enterprise   A difficult or risky project.

frontier   The edge of the settled part of a country.

inaugural address   A speech given at the beginning of a president's term in office.

mochila   A lightweight cover for a saddle, with pouches to hold the mail.

populace   Group of citizens of a town or city.

precipice   A very steep place.

reenact   To perform again.

relay   Passing something along or completing something in stages.

scribe   Someone hired to write something down.

stagecoach   A wagon pulled by horses that runs on a regular schedule and carries mail, supplies, or people.

telegram   A message sent by telegraph.

telegraph   An electric device that can send messages, usually in code, through a wire.

Union   The Northern states that remained a part of the United States during the Civil War.

wiry   Thin but strong.

FOR MORE INFORMATION

National Pony Express Association
P.O. Box 236
Pollock Pines, CA 95726

Pony Express National Museum
914 Penn Street
St. Joseph, MO 64503
(800) 530-5930
Web site: http://www.ponyexpress.org

St. Joseph Museum Inc.
P.O. Box 128
St. Joseph, MO 64502-0128
(800) 530-8866
Web site: http://www.stjosephmuseum.org

Wells Fargo History Museum
420 Montgomery Street
San Francisco, CA 94163
(415) 396-2619
Web site: http://www.wellsfargohistory.com/museums/
    sfmuseum.html

Web Sites

Due to the changing nature of Internet links, the Rosen Publishing Group, Inc., has developed an online list of Web sites related to the subject of this book. This site is updated regularly. Please use this link to access the list:

http://www.rosenlinks.com/psah/poex

FOR FURTHER READING

Jensen, Lee. *The Pony Express.* New York: Grosset & Dunlap, 1955.

Moody, Ralph. *Riders of the Pony Express.* Boston: Houghton Mifflin, 1958.

Riddle, John. *The Pony Express.* Broomall, PA: Mason Crest Publishers, 2003.

Stein, R. Conrad. *The Story of the Pony Express.* Chicago: Children's Press, 1981.

Van der Linde, Laurel. *The Pony Express.* New York: New Discovery Books, 1993.

BIBLIOGRAPHY

Billington, Ray Allen. *Westward Expansion: A History of the American Frontier.* Third Edition. New York: The Macmillan Company, 1967.

Bloss, Roy S. *Pony Express: The Great Gamble.* Berkeley, CA: Howell-North, 1959.

Chapman, Arthur. *The Pony Express: The Record of a Romantic Adventure in Business.* New York: Cooper Square Publishers, Inc., 1971.

Delano, Alonzo. "Life on the Plains and Among the Diggings, in California As I Saw It: First-Person Narratives of California's Early Years, 1849–1900." Library of Congress. October 1998. Retrieved July 5, 2003 (http://memory.loc.gov/cgi-bin/query/D?calbkbib:2:./temp/~ammem_MxEK::).

Ellis, Jerry. *Bareback!: One Man's Journey Along the Pony Express Trail.* New York: Delacorte Press, 1993.

Godfrey, Anthony. "Pony Express National Historic Trail: Historic Resource Study." U.S. Department of the Interior, National Park Service. August 1994. Retrieved June 23, 2002 (http://www.nps.gov/poex/hrs/hrs.htm).

Harness, Cheryl. *They're Off!: The Story of the Pony Express.* New York: Simon & Schuster Books for Young Readers, 1996.

Jensen, Lee. *The Pony Express.* New York: Grosset & Dunlap, 1955.

Kroll, Steven. *Pony Express!* New York: Scholastic, Inc. 1996.

Moody, Ralph. *Riders of the Pony Express.* Boston: Houghton Mifflin, 1958.

Riddle, John. *The Pony Express.* Broomall, PA: Mason Crest Publishers, 2003.

Settle, Raymond W., and Mary Lund Settle. *Saddles and Spurs: The Pony Express Saga.* Harrisburg, PA: The Stackpole Company, 1955.

Smith, Waddell F., ed. *The Story of the Pony Express.* San Rafael, CA: Pony Express History and Art Gallery, 1960.

Stein, R. Conrad. *The Story of the Pony Express.* Chicago: Children's Press, 1981.

Stewart, Alex. *Sending a Letter.* New York: Franklin Watts, 1999.

Twain, Mark. *Roughing It.* New York: New American Library of World Literature, 1962.

Van der Linde, Laurel. *The Pony Express.* New York: New Discovery Books, 1993.

PRIMARY SOURCE IMAGE LIST

Page 5: Naval and military map of the United States, showing Pony Express route. Created by John Calvin Smith. Engraved by J. M. Atwood. Published in Philadelphia in 1862. Housed in the Library of Congress, Washington, D.C.

Page 11: Photograph of mail route milestone, located on State Route 9 in Spencer, Worcester County, Massachusetts. Housed in the Library of Congress.

Page 13: *Post Office, San Francisco, California: A Faithful Representation of the Crowds Daily Applying at that Office for Letters and Newspapers.* Lithograph created by William Endicott and Co. in 1850.

Page 14: *The Way They Go to California.* Lithograph created by Nathaniel Currier circa 1849. Housed in the Bancroft Library at the University of California, Berkeley.

Page 16: Portrait of Aaron Brown. Engraving by J. C. Buttre. Housed in the Library of Congress.

Page 19: Photographic portraits of William Waddell, William Russell, and Alexander Majors. Housed in the Pony Express National Memorial, St. Joseph, Missouri.

Page 21: Poster advertising Buffalo Bill's Wild West and Congress of Rough Riders of the World Show. Printed in the nineteenth century by Courier Lithograph Co.

Page 23: Photograph of Frank E. Webner on his horse. Taken in 1861.

Page 24: Poster advertising the Pony Express. Created circa 1860. From Wells Fargo Archives.

Page 27: Reprinted page of *St. Joseph Daily Gazette,* Pony Express Edition. Original printed on April 3, 1860. From the St. Joseph Museum.

Page 28: Facsimile of election news carried by the Pony Express. November 8, 1860.

Page 30: *Changing Mounts at Pony Express Station.* Engraving by Frederic Remington, circa 1895.

Page 32: Illustration of Warren Upson riding during a snowstorm. Housed in the Bancroft Library at the University of California, Berkeley.

Page 37: Photograph of Johnny Frye. From the St. Joseph Museum.

Page 38: Photograph of Billy Fisher. Taken circa 1860. Housed in the Pony Express Museum, St. Joseph.

Page 40: Page from draft of Abraham Lincoln's first inaugural address. March 4, 1861. Housed in the Library of Congress.

Page 42: Photograph showing a Pony Express station. Taken by William Henry Jackson. Housed at the Harold B. Lee Library at Brigham Young University, Provo, Utah.

Page 45: Photograph of a mail station in the Salt Lake Valley. Taken by Edward Martin circa 1860. Housed in the Harold B. Lee Library at Brigham Young University.

Page 47: Portrait of Winnemucca, Paiute chief. Photographed in 1880.

Page 48: *Indians Attacking United States Mail Coach.* Illustrated in 1860. From Wells Fargo Archives.

Page 53: Announcement for the end of the Pony Express. Printed in the *San Francisco Evening Bulletin* on October 26, 1861. From Wells Fargo Archives.

Page 54: U.S. stamp commemorating the Pony Express. Photographed by Leonard de Selva in 1960.

INDEX

About the Author

Simone Payment has a degree in psychology from Cornell University and a master's degree in elementary education from Wheelock College. She is the author of seven books for young adults.

Acknowledgments

The author would like to thank Marina Lang for her suggestions on the manuscript. She would also like to thank the reference librarians of the Wakefield (Massachusetts) Public Library for their assistance.

Photo Credits

Cover, p. 16 Library of Congress, Prints and Photographs Division; pp. 1, 48 Culver Pictures, Inc.; p. 5 Library of Congress, Geography and Map Division; p. 11 Library of Congress, Prints and Photographs Division, HABS, MASS, 14-LEIC, 3-1; pp. 13, 21, 23, 47, 53 © Corbis; p. 14 courtesy of the Bancroft Library, University of California, Berkeley; pp. 19, 27, 37, 38 St. Joseph Museum Inc., St. Joseph, Missouri; pp. 24, 28, 30, 34 © Bettmann/Corbis; pp. 32, 51 General Research Division, New York Public Library, Astor, Lenox, and Tilden Foundations; p. 40 Library of Congress, Manuscript Division; pp. 42, 45 Special Collections, Harold B. Lee Library, Brigham Young University; p. 54 © Leonard de Selva/Corbis.

Designer: Nelson Sá; **Editor:** Christine Poolos;
Photo Researcher: Peter Tomlinson